An Easy Guide to Financial Freedom:

How to Live a Life of Abundance on a Low Income

Flawless Dave

Table of Contents

Embracing the Abundance Mindset

Living a Life of Abundance on a Low Income: Your Journey Continues!

I. Introduction

Definition of Abundance

Let's explore the amazing world of living a life of abundance on a low income. But first, let's understand what "abundance" means in this context. Abundance isn't just about having lots of money or luxurious items. It's a mindset and a way of life that allows us to experience a fulfilling and prosperous life, regardless of our financial situation.

Imagine waking up each morning feeling content and grateful for the blessings in your life. Abundance is about finding joy in the small things, cherishing the relationships you have, and being present in the moments that matter most. It's about recognizing the wealth of possibilities and opportunities that are around you, even on a limited budget.

You may not have the latest gadgets or a fancy car, but if you have a roof over your head, food on the table, and people who love and support you, you're already experiencing abundance.

Living a life of abundance on a low income means changing our outlook from what we don't have to what we do have. It's about being resourceful, creative, and making the most of the resources available to us. It may not be easy, but it's definitely possible, and it starts with cultivating the right attitude.

Abundance is like a garden. You can either focus on the barren patches and complain about the lack of flowers, or you can nurture the seeds you have, water them with gratitude and positivity, and watch as they blossom into a beautiful and vibrant landscape.

I want to emphasize that embracing abundance doesn't mean ignoring financial responsibilities or pretending that money doesn't matter. Instead, it's about being smart with your finances, finding ways to save and earn more, and aligning your spending with what truly brings you joy and fulfillment.

Living an abundant life is a wonderful way to experience joy and fulfillment. It's not just about having material possessions; it's about feeling a deep sense of well-being and happiness in all aspects of life. Here are some of the incredible benefits of embracing abundance:

Gratitude and Contentment:

When you open your heart to abundance, you become more appreciative of the small things that bring joy. You find contentment in simple pleasures, like savoring a warm cup of tea, spending quality time with loved ones, or witnessing a beautiful sunset. By focusing on what you have rather than what you lack, you'll discover that happiness is not just an end goal but a continuous state of being.

Mental and Emotional Well-Being:

Living abundantly is closely linked to positive thinking and a healthier mindset. When you focus on gratitude and abundance, you reduce stress, anxiety, and negative thought patterns. Your mind becomes a more nurturing space, allowing you to handle challenges with greater resilience and optimism.

Stronger Relationships and Connection:

Abundance extends to the richness of relationships you cultivate. When you appreciate the people around you and cherish their presence, your connections deepen. You'll find that your bonds with family, friends, and even new acquaintances become more meaningful, fostering a sense of community and support.

Creativity and Resourcefulness:

Living an abundant life encourages you to tap into your creativity and resourcefulness. You learn to make the most out of what you have, finding innovative solutions to challenges. Just like an artist who transforms ordinary materials into a masterpiece, you'll see opportunities where others might only see limitations.

Empowerment and Personal Growth:

Abundance empowers you to take control of your life and actively pursue your goals and dreams. As you believe in your abilities and the abundant opportunities around you, you'll feel more confident in taking calculated risks and stepping outside your comfort zone. This newfound courage propels your personal growth and self-discovery.

Improved Physical Health:

An abundant life often leads to healthier habits. When you focus on nourishing your body and mind, you may find yourself making better food choices, engaging in regular exercise, and prioritizing self-care. These positive lifestyle changes can contribute to improved overall well-being and vitality.

Generosity and Compassion:

Living abundantly opens your heart to acts of kindness and generosity. When you feel abundant, you naturally want to share your blessings with others. Acts of giving and compassion not only benefit those on the receiving end but also bring a profound sense of fulfillment and interconnectedness.

Attraction of Positive Opportunities:

Abundance is like a magnetic force that attracts positive opportunities and experiences into your life. When you radiate positivity and gratitude, you become more open to new possibilities, collaborations, and synchronicities. Doors that seemed closed before may suddenly swing wide open.

Living an abundant life is a mindset shift that brings a multitude of blessings into your existence. It's a journey of self-discovery and personal transformation, where you realize that the key to abundance lies within you. Embrace abundance and you'll find yourself waking up each morning with a sense of excitement and joy, knowing that your life is filled with richness and fulfillment.

II. Strategies for Living an Abundant Life on a Low Income

Budgeting

Budgeting—a powerful tool that can help you live an abundant life on a low income. You might think budgeting is intimidating, but it's not as scary as it seems. It's like having a magic wand that gives you control over your finances and makes your money work for you!

So, what is budgeting? It's simply creating a plan for your money. It's like having a roadmap that guides you on how to use your income wisely, so you can cover all your essential expenses and still have room for the things that bring you joy.

Imagine this: You have a jar full of marbles, and each marble represents a dollar you earn. Instead of spending these marbles randomly, budgeting is about sorting them into different jars—each jar representing a specific spending category, like rent, groceries, transportation, savings, and entertainment. By organizing your marbles, you can see where your money is going and make sure you don't run out before the month ends.

Here's why budgeting is so important for living an abundant life on a low income:

Financial Awareness:

Budgeting gives you a clear view of your financial situation. You'll know exactly how much money you have, how much you spend, and where you can make changes to save more. It's like turning on a light for your finances, getting rid of any doubt, and giving you the power to make smart decisions.

Smart Spending Habits:

With a budget in place, you become more aware of your spending habits. You'll find out where you might be overspending and discover ways to cut back without sacrificing your happiness. By optimizing your spending, you'll have more marbles left for the things that really matter to you.

Financial Goals:

Budgeting helps you set and reach financial goals. Whether it's saving for an emergency fund, paying off debts, or planning a dream vacation, a budget shows you how to use your marbles towards your objectives. It's like having a roadmap to your dreams!

Let's use an example to bring budgeting to life:

Meet Amy, a young professional with a limited income. She loves going out with friends but often finds herself running out of money before the end of the month. Amy decides to give budgeting a try.

Step 1: Amy tracks her income and expenses for a month. She notices that a big portion of her marbles is going towards eating out at restaurants.

Step 2: Amy creates a budget for the next month, allocating a certain number of marbles to each spending category. She decides to reduce eating out and reallocates those marbles to a savings jar.

Step 3: With her budget in place, Amy starts bringing homemade lunches to work and invites friends over for potluck dinners instead of going to expensive restaurants.

Result: At the end of the month, Amy finds she has more marbles left over than she's had in a long time. Not only is she proud of her newfound financial discipline, but she also realizes that budgeting hasn't taken away her happiness—it has actually given her the ability to make smarter choices and have more marbles for meaningful experiences.

So, my friend, budgeting is your secret weapon for financial freedom and living abundantly on a low income. It's about making every marble count and aligning your spending with what truly brings you joy.

There's a game-changing strategy that can help you find ways to increase your income. Now, we all know that money isn't the key to happiness, but having a little extra in your pocket can certainly open up a world of possibilities and opportunities.

So, how can you boost your income? Let's put on our detective hats and explore the world of income-boosting possibilities! Here are five ideas to get you started:

1. **Unleash Your Talents and Skills:** Think about what makes you unique—your talents, skills, and passions. Maybe you're a gifted writer, a talented artist, or a tech-savvy whiz. Consider how you can turn these abilities into a side hustle or freelance gig. For example, if you love writing, you could offer content creation services to businesses or start a blog and monetize it through ads and sponsored content.

2. **Tap into the Gig Economy:** The gig economy is buzzing with opportunities. From ride-sharing and food delivery services to online tutoring and virtual assisting, there's a gig for almost every skill. Embrace the flexibility and convenience of gig work, and you might find yourself with some extra marbles in your jar.

3. **Monetize Your Hobbies:** What if you could turn your hobbies into a money-making venture? Let's say you're an

avid photographer—consider selling your photos online or offering photography sessions to friends and family. Whether it's crafting, gardening, or baking, explore ways to share your passion and earn an income from it.

4. **Embrace the Power of the Internet:** The internet is a treasure trove of opportunities. From starting an online store and selling products to offering online courses or consulting services, the digital world opens doors to a global audience. Embrace the online realm, and you'll discover a vast marketplace for your skills and expertise.

5. **Network and Collaborate:** Connections are golden. Reach out to your network and let people know you're looking for extra income opportunities. You never know when someone might need your help or bc aware of an exciting venture you can join. Collaborations can be a win-win for everyone involved.

Let's take Alex as an example of income-boosting success. Alex had a passion for health and fitness, but they were already working a full-time job. So, they decided to become a certified personal trainer on weekends. They started offering personal training sessions to friends and family at a discounted rate, building a solid client base and gaining experience. Soon, word-of-mouth spread, and they started getting referrals from satisfied clients. Before they knew it, they were running a successful side business, helping people achieve their fitness goals while also enjoying a significant boost in income.

The takeaway is this: Increasing your income doesn't have to mean working harder or sacrificing your passion. It's about recognizing your unique strengths and leveraging them to create additional income streams that align with your interests and skills.

So, my friend, let your creativity and resourcefulness shine as you explore ways to boost your income. The more marbles you add to your jar, the more opportunities you'll have to live abundantly and experience the richness life has to offer.

Making Smart Financial Decisions

Let's chat about one of the most important abilities for living a prosperous life on a low income—making wise financial decisions. Think of it as your superpower that will help you make the most of the marbles in your jar!

So, what exactly are smart financial decisions? They are like a compass that guides you through the twists and turns of your financial journey, helping you move towards success and abundance. Making smart financial decisions is about being mindful, informed, and proactive with your money.

Imagine this: You're walking through a marketplace filled with attractive displays, bright signs, and a variety of products. Smart financial decisions are like having a discerning eye that helps you pick out the best deals, avoid impulse buys, and make choices that are in line with your financial goals.

Here's why making smart financial decisions is so important:

1. Maximizing Your Marbles:

With a limited income, every marble matters. Smart financial decisions allow you to get the most value out of each marble, so you can cover your essential expenses and still have some left for the things that bring you joy.

2. Debt Avoidance and Reduction:

By making wise choices, you can avoid unnecessary debt and work towards reducing any existing debt. This frees up more of your marbles for building a secure financial future.

3. Creating a Safety Net:

Life is full of surprises, and having a safety net in place is essential. Making smart financial decisions means setting aside some marbles for an emergency fund, ensuring you're prepared for unexpected expenses.

4. Building Wealth for the Future:

Smart financial decisions aren't just about surviving the present; they're about thriving in the future. By making strategic investments and saving for long-term goals, you're planting the seeds for future abundance.

Now, let's take a look at Emily, the queen of smart financial decisions:

Emily had always dreamed of traveling the world, but she thought it was impossible on her low income. However, instead of giving up on her dreams, she made smart financial decisions to make them a reality.

Step 1: Emily researched budget-friendly travel destinations, opting for places with low living costs and plenty of free or affordable activities.

Step 2: Instead of eating out every day, Emily started cooking at home and saving the money she would have spent on dining out.

Step 3: She cut down on other discretionary expenses, like expensive coffee drinks and unnecessary shopping sprees, putting those marbles into a dedicated travel fund.

Result: After a few months of smart financial decisions, Emily found she had enough marbles to embark on her first international adventure. She was able to experience new cultures, savor delicious foods, and create unforgettable memories—all without breaking the bank.

The takeaway is this: Smart financial decisions are like stepping stones that lead you to a life of abundance. It's about being aware of how you use your marbles and making choices that are in line with your values and goals.

So, let's make a pact to be champions of smart financial decisions. Together, we'll sharpen our financial skills, take advantage of opportunities to save and invest wisely, and create a future where financial abundance is not just a dream but a beautiful reality.

Practicing Gratitude

Let's discuss a transformative approach that can make your life a beacon of positivity and abundance—practicing gratitude. Gratitude is like a magical lens that allows you to see the abundance that already exists in your life, even on a low income. It's a powerful tool that can fill your heart with joy and appreciation for the riches you have, both big and small.

So, what is gratitude? Gratitude is the art of recognizing and being thankful for the blessings, goodness, and positive aspects of your life. It's like putting on a pair of special glasses that let you see the silver lining in every situation.

Imagine this: You wake up every morning and take a moment to think about the things you're grateful for—a cozy bed, a loving family, or the beauty of nature outside your window. With each expression of gratitude, you fill your heart with warmth and positivity, setting the tone for a day filled with abundance.

Here's why practicing gratitude is essential for living an abundant life on a low income:

1. Changing Your Perspective:

Gratitude is a powerful perspective changer. When you focus on the things you're grateful for, you shift your attention away from what you lack and towards what you have. Suddenly, your marbles feel more substantial, and you realize that abundance goes beyond material possessions.

2. Finding Joy in the Little Things:

Gratitude allows you to find joy in the smallest of moments. Whether it's a kind word from a friend, a beautiful sunset, or a hot cup of tea on a chilly day, these moments become precious gems that enrich your life.

3. Building Resilience:

Practicing gratitude doesn't mean ignoring challenges; it means finding strength and resilience amidst them. When you're grateful for the lessons learned through difficult times, you become better equipped to handle future challenges with grace and determination.

Now, let's meet Sarah, a gratitude practitioner and a beacon of positivity:

Sarah was a single mom raising two kids on a tight budget. Instead of feeling overwhelmed by financial constraints, she embraced gratitude as a way of life.

Step 1: Every evening, Sarah and her kids gathered around the dinner table to share three things they were grateful for that day. This simple practice filled their home with love and positivity.

Step 2: Whenever Sarah felt stressed about money, she took a moment to appreciate the support and love she received from her children, friends, and community.

Step 3: Sarah started a gratitude journal, writing down things she was thankful for each day. She noticed that even on tough days, there were always silver linings to be grateful for.

Result: Sarah's home became a haven of abundance and joy. She and her kids found contentment in simple pleasures, like reading books from the library or having picnics in the park. They cherished their time together and felt rich in love and connection.

The takeaway is this: Practicing gratitude is a powerful way to unlock the hidden treasures of abundance in your life. It's about cultivating a mindset of appreciation and savoring the richness of every moment.

So, let's learn to make gratitude a cornerstone of our abundant life journey. As we cultivate a heart full of gratitude, we'll find that our jar of marbles feels fuller and more valuable than ever before.

III. Practical Tips for Living an Abundant Life on a Low Income

Prioritizing Your Needs

Prioritizing your needs is like having a compass that points you in the right direction to make decisions that reflect your values and bring you true satisfaction. So, what does it mean to prioritize your needs? It's about recognizing what is most important to you and focusing your resources on those essential areas. It's like being the captain of your financial ship, guiding it towards calmer waters and avoiding unnecessary storms.

Let's say you're planning a dream vacation, but you're also dealing with mounting bills. Prioritizing your needs means evaluating which one is more important for your overall well-being. Maybe the vacation can wait while you take care of your financial responsibilities first.

Here's why prioritizing your needs is essential for living an abundant life on a low income:

1. Avoiding Financial Stress:

When you prioritize your needs, you reduce financial stress. By taking care of the most important expenses first, you create a sense of stability and control over your finances.

2. Creating Balance and Harmony:

Prioritizing helps you find a balance between spending on what you need and indulging in what you want. It allows you to enjoy life's pleasures without sacrificing your long-term financial well-being.

3. Fostering Gratitude and Contentment:

By focusing on your true needs, you develop a sense of gratitude for what you have. You'll find contentment in having your essential needs met and feel less inclined to chase after fleeting desires.

Now, let's meet Mark, a master of prioritizing his needs:

Mark had always dreamed of owning a new car, but he was also carrying some credit card debt. Instead of giving in to the temptation of a new car, Mark decided to prioritize his financial health.

Step 1: Mark made a list of his essential needs—paying off his credit card debt, building an emergency fund, and saving for future goals.

Step 2: He created a budget that allocated a significant portion of his resources to tackling his debt and building savings.

Step 3: Mark resisted the temptation to splurge on unnecessary expenses and focused on his financial priorities.

Result: After a few months of prioritizing his needs, Mark paid off his credit card debt and built a substantial emergency fund. Not only did he feel a sense of accomplishment, but he also felt more in control of his finances, making him truly abundant in peace of mind.

The takeaway is this: Prioritizing your needs is a game-changer for living an abundant life. It's about making conscious choices that align with your financial goals and values.

As we focus our resources on what truly matters, we'll find that abundance is not just about having more, but about feeling fulfilled and content with what we have.

Making the Most of What You Have

Living an abundant life on a low income is possible with a simple tip: make the most of what you have! It's like unlocking the hidden potential in each of your marbles and discovering the magic of resourcefulness.

So, what does making the most of what you have mean? It's about tapping into your creativity and finding innovative ways to use the resources at your disposal. It's like being an alchemist who turns ordinary materials into extraordinary treasures.

Let's say you open your kitchen pantry and find a few basic ingredients—a can of beans, some rice, and a few vegetables. Making the most of what you have means transforming these humble ingredients into a delicious and nutritious meal that fills your belly with satisfaction.

Here's why making the most of what you have is so important for living an abundant life on a low income:

1. Stretching Your Marbles:

By making the most of what you have, you stretch your marbles further than you thought possible. You'll find that a little creativity can turn ordinary experiences into extraordinary moments.

2. Empowering Resourcefulness:

Resourcefulness is a superpower. When you embrace making the most of what you have, you tap into your inner genius and discover unique solutions to challenges.

3. Celebrating Simplicity:

Making the most of what you have teaches you to appreciate the beauty in simplicity. You'll find joy in the little things and feel abundant in the richness of each moment.

Let's look at Lisa, the queen of making the most of what she has:

Lisa loved fashion, but she had a limited clothing budget. Instead of feeling deprived, she embraced the challenge of creating stylish outfits from her existing wardrobe.

Step 1: Lisa organized her closet and discovered hidden gems—a classic white shirt she could dress up or down, a versatile blazer that went with everything, and a statement necklace that transformed any outfit.

Step 2: She learned to mix and match her clothing items, creating different combinations that looked fresh and stylish each time.

Step 3: Lisa added a few affordable accessories to her collection, like scarves and belts, to give her outfits a new twist.

Result: Lisa became known for her impeccable style, and people were amazed at how she always looked so put together. She realized that making the most of what she had not only saved her marbles but also unlocked a world of fashion creativity.

The takeaway is this: Making the most of what you have is a powerful mindset that turns limitations into opportunities. It's about recognizing the abundance in simplicity and using your resources in ingenious ways.

Making the most of free resources is a great way to unlock a wealth of opportunities on your journey to an abundant life on a low income. It's like discovering a secret garden filled with valuable tools and knowledge, all available to you without spending a penny.

So, what does taking advantage of free resources mean? It's about tapping into the wealth of knowledge, support, and experiences available to you without any financial cost. It's like having a VIP pass to a world of possibilities, waiting for you to explore and grow.

Imagine this: You step into a beautiful library filled with books, courses, workshops, and knowledgeable mentors—all free of charge. Taking advantage of free resources means immersing yourself in this wealth of knowledge to enhance your skills, expand your horizons, and nurture your passions.

Here's why taking advantage of free resources is so important for living an abundant life on a low income:

1. Self-Development:

Free resources give you the chance to invest in your personal growth without spending a dime. Whether it's learning new skills, exploring hobbies, or gaining knowledge, you'll find endless opportunities for self-improvement.

2. Building Your Network:

By accessing free resources, you can connect with like-minded individuals and build a supportive community. Networking opens doors to collaboration, mentorship, and new friendships.

3. Saving Your Money for What Matters:

Taking advantage of free resources allows you to save your money for essential expenses and meaningful experiences. It's like having an abundance of tools at your disposal without depleting your financial resources.

Let's meet Mike, the master of leveraging free resources:

Mike had a passion for photography, but he couldn't afford expensive camera gear or photography courses. Instead of giving up on his dream, he explored free resources to develop his skills.

Step 1: Mike joined online photography forums, where experienced photographers shared tips and critiques.

Step 2: He discovered free photography tutorials on YouTube and blogs, learning various techniques and editing tips.

Step 3: Mike found local photography groups that organized free photowalks and meetups, where he gained valuable practical experience and made friends with other photography enthusiasts.

Result: Mike's photography skills blossomed, and he started receiving compliments on his stunning photos. By taking advantage of free resources, he turned his passion into a flourishing hobby without spending a fortune.

The takeaway is this: Making the most of free resources is like having a treasure chest of opportunities at your fingertips. It's about embracing the wealth of knowledge and support available to you and investing in your growth and happiness.

As we immerse ourselves in this abundance of knowledge and experiences, we'll discover that our money can create a life filled with learning, growth, and fulfillment.

Investing in Yourself

Investing in yourself is an incredible way to supercharge your life with abundance. It's like planting the seeds of growth and empowerment that will blossom into a magnificent garden of opportunities, even on a low income.

So, what does investing in yourself mean? It's about recognizing your worth and dedicating time, effort, and sometimes even a few marbles to nurture your personal and professional development. It's like watering a beautiful plant—when you invest in yourself, you nourish your potential to blossom and thrive.

Imagine this: You hold a precious seed in your hand—the seed of your dreams, passions, and potential. By investing in yourself, you provide the perfect environment for that seed to grow into a thriving and abundant future.

Here's why investing in yourself is essential for living an abundant life on a low income:

1. Unlocking Your Full Potential:

Investing in yourself allows you to unlock your full potential and tap into talents and abilities you might not even know you have. It's like uncovering hidden treasures within you.

2. Generating Opportunities:

By developing your skills and knowledge, you create opportunities for personal growth and career advancement.

Investing in yourself opens doors to new possibilities you might not have imagined before.

3. **Building Resilience:**

Investing in yourself equips you with tools and knowledge that make you more resilient in the face of challenges. You become better prepared to navigate obstacles and bounce back stronger.

Let's take a look at Jenna, a shining example of self-investment:

Jenna had a passion for writing, but she felt hesitant about pursuing it seriously due to her low income. Instead of giving in to self-doubt, she decided to invest in herself.

Step 1: Jenna signed up for free online writing courses and attended workshops to improve her writing skills.

Step 2: She set aside a small portion of her marbles each month to buy books on writing and storytelling.

Step 3: Jenna joined a local writing group, where she received feedback on her work and connected with other aspiring writers.

Result: After months of self-investment, Jenna felt more confident in her writing abilities. She started submitting her stories to publications and competitions. One day, her talent was recognized, and she received an offer to write a series of articles for a popular magazine—a dream come true!

The takeaway is this: Investing in yourself is a profound act of self-love and belief. It's about nurturing your dreams and passions, even with limited resources, and trusting that those investments will yield abundant returns.

As we dedicate time and effort to nourishing our growth, we'll witness a beautiful transformation taking place—one that propels us towards an abundant life filled with fulfillment and success. Get ready to water the seeds of your potential and watch as your marbles create a lush garden of possibilities!

IV. Mastering Money Management

Let's dive into the world of mastering money management and explore a crucial aspect that will give you financial prowess—developing smart spending habits. Think of it as a secret recipe that will turn your marbles into a feast of abundance and financial freedom.

So, what are smart spending habits? They're like golden keys that open the door to financial success. Smart spending habits are all about making mindful and intentional choices with your marbles, so they serve your long-term goals and lead you to a life of prosperity.

Imagine this: You're strolling through a marketplace filled with attractive displays and flashy sales. With smart spending habits, you become a savvy shopper, carefully selecting the items that bring real value to your life.

Here's why developing smart spending habits is essential for mastering money management:

1. **Aligning Spending with Your Values:**

Smart spending habits make sure that your marbles are spent on things that are in line with your values and priorities. It's about investing in experiences and items that bring joy and fulfillment.

2. **Building a Solid Financial Foundation:**

By making wise spending choices, you create a strong financial foundation. You'll have more marbles available for emergencies, savings, and investments, setting you up for a brighter future.

3. **Avoiding the Trap of Impulse Purchases:**

Smart spending habits help you resist the temptation of impulse purchases. You'll think twice before splurging on something that might bring temporary happiness but won't contribute to your long-term well-being.

Now, let's meet Alex, the master of smart spending habits:

Alex loved technology and gadgets, but they often found themselves buying the latest gadgets without considering the long-term impact on their finances. That's when Alex decided to develop smart spending habits.

Step 1: Alex created a budget, allocating a specific portion of their marbles to discretionary spending, including gadgets.

Step 2: Before making any purchase, Alex researched and compared prices to find the best deals.

Step 3: Alex practiced the "24-hour rule"—whenever they wanted to buy a gadget, they waited 24 hours before making the decision. This helped avoid impulse purchases.

Result: With smart spending habits in place, Alex found they were spending less on gadgets and had more marbles to put towards experiences like travel and investing in courses to advance their career.

The takeaway is this: Developing smart spending habits is like having a financial compass that guides you towards a life of abundance. It's about being intentional with your marbles and making choices that align with your financial goals and values.

Understanding the Importance of an Emergency Fund

Having a solid understanding of money management is essential, and one of the most important aspects of this is having an emergency fund. Think of it as a superhero shield that safeguards your financial stability and provides a safety net in times of crisis. An emergency fund is like a special jar where you store a portion of your money to use only in emergencies. It's your fortress of financial security, ready to come to the rescue when life throws unexpected curveballs.

For example, if you're on a grand adventure and you encounter a roadblock such as a surprise medical bill, a car repair, or a job loss, your emergency fund can help you overcome the obstacle. Here are three reasons why having an emergency fund is so important for mastering money management:

1. Financial Safety Net:

An emergency fund is your safety net in times of crisis. It prevents you from having to rely on high-interest loans or credit cards to cover unexpected expenses, which could lead to a spiral of debt.

2. Peace of Mind:

Having an emergency fund in place gives you peace of mind knowing that you're prepared for life's uncertainties. You'll sleep better at night, knowing that your finances are secure and protected.

3. Flexibility and Freedom:

Having an emergency fund gives you the freedom to make choices without financial fear. It empowers you to seize opportunities, navigate unexpected challenges, and embrace life with confidence.

Let's look at Sarah, an example of someone who understood the importance of an emergency fund. When her car broke down, she had to rely on her credit card to cover the repairs, resulting in a hefty debt. After this experience, Sarah realized the importance of an emergency fund and committed to building one. She set a monthly savings goal and created a separate account for her emergency fund. She treated her emergency fund as a priority and contributed to it consistently, even if it meant cutting back on non-essential expenses. When Sarah faced an unexpected medical expense a few months later, she was relieved to have her emergency fund and used it to cover the bill, avoiding any financial strain.

The takeaway is this: An emergency fund is like a guardian angel for your finances. It's not a matter of "if" unexpected events happen; it's a matter of "when." By understanding the importance of an emergency fund, you're prepared to face whatever life throws your way.

Saving for the Future: Retirement and Long-Term Goals

Securing your future is an essential part of managing your finances and setting yourself up for a life of financial abundance and security. It's like planting a garden of dreams, where each marble you save becomes a tiny seed that will sprout into a beautiful tree of opportunities.

Think of it as sowing the seeds of prosperity that will grow into a bountiful harvest, ensuring your marbles work tirelessly to create the life you desire. Saving for the future is about nurturing your long-term financial goals and giving them the space to flourish.

Imagine this: You're looking at the horizon, envisioning a future where you're free to pursue your passions, enjoy financial independence, and experience the joys of retirement. Saving for the future is the compass that guides you towards that vision, step by step.

Here's why saving for the future is so important for mastering money management:

1. Financial Security in Retirement:

By setting aside marbles for retirement, you can ensure that when you reach the golden years of life, you'll have enough to sustain yourself comfortably and enjoy the fruits of your labor.

2. Achieving Long-Term Dreams:

By saving for long-term goals, like buying a home, starting a business, or traveling the world, you empower yourself to turn those dreams into reality.

3. **Compound Interest Magic:**

Saving for the future allows your marbles to work their magic through compound interest. The earlier you start, the more your money grows over time.

Let's look at Tom, the master of saving for the future:

Tom had a dream of retiring early and traveling the world, but he knew he needed to save wisely to achieve that dream.

Step 1: Tom set up a retirement savings account and a separate savings account for his long-term travel goal.

Step 2: He automated his savings, so a portion of his income went directly into these accounts each month.

Step 3: Tom lived below his means, avoiding unnecessary expenses and directing more marbles towards his savings.

Result: Years later, Tom's retirement savings had grown significantly due to the power of compound interest. He retired comfortably and embarked on his dream travel adventure, confident that he had prepared well for the future.

The lesson here is that saving for the future is like planting seeds of financial freedom and empowerment. It's not about depriving yourself of the present, but about nurturing your dreams and providing for your future self.

As we sow the seeds of prosperity and watch our marbles grow, we'll be well-prepared to embrace a life of abundance, joy, and fulfillment. Get ready to tend to your financial garden and witness the remarkable transformation it brings to your life and future!

V. Pursuing Personal Development and Learning Opportunities

Free and Low-Cost Resources for Education
Free and Low-Cost Resources for Education
Let's embark on an exciting journey to pursue personal growth and open ourselves up to a world of endless knowledge and development. Let's uncover a wealth of free and low-cost educational resources that will nourish your mind and give you the power to reach new heights.

So, what are these free and low-cost educational resources? Imagine a huge library where each book, course, and workshop is a golden ticket to broaden your horizons. Free and low-cost educational resources are the magical keys that open the doors to learning without breaking the bank.

Imagine this: You're standing at the entrance of a magical garden, filled with chances to explore new topics, master new abilities, and uncover hidden passions. With free and low-cost educational resources, you're the captain of your own growth, guiding yourself towards a future of endless possibilities.

Here's why embracing free and low-cost educational resources is essential for pursuing personal development:

1. **Accessible Learning for Everyone:**

With free and low-cost resources, education becomes accessible and available to all. It doesn't matter where you come from or how much money you have; the world of knowledge is open to you.

2. Empowerment Through Skills:

Free and low-cost resources give you the skills to increase your confidence and open up career opportunities. Learning becomes a ladder that propels you towards success.

3. Fueling Lifelong Curiosity:

When education is affordable, you're encouraged to explore a wide range of subjects and follow your curiosity. Learning becomes a lifelong journey that keeps your mind sharp and engaged.

Now, let's meet Lisa, the champion of free and low-cost educational resources:

Lisa was passionate about graphic design, but she couldn't afford to attend an expensive design school. Instead, she looked for free and low-cost resources to nurture her talent.

Step 1: Lisa joined online platforms that offer free courses and tutorials on graphic design.

Step 2: She took part in webinars and workshops hosted by design professionals, often at little to no cost.

Step 3: Lisa joined online design communities where she could collaborate, get feedback, and learn from other designers.

Result: With dedication and the power of affordable education, Lisa honed her graphic design skills. She became proficient in various design software and eventually landed a well-paying freelance job—a dream come true!

The takeaway is this: Embracing free and low-cost educational resources is like unlocking the door to a world of knowledge and personal growth. It's about giving yourself the power to reach new heights, even without expensive tuition fees.

Investing in Your Skills and Talents

Let's embark on a journey of self-improvement to unlock your full potential and bring out the strength of your abilities and talents.

So, what does investing in your skills and talents mean? Visualize yourself as a sculptor, chipping away at a block of marble to create a stunning statue. Investing in your skills and talents is like sharpening your tools and refining your craft, so you can create masterpieces that leave the world in awe.

Imagine this: You stand on a grand stage, displaying your talents to an enthusiastic audience. With every song you sing, every brushstroke you paint, or every line of code you write, you're a living example of the power of investing in yourself.

Here's why investing in your skills and talents is essential for pursuing personal development:

1. Uncovering Your Unique Potential:

Investing in your skills and talents allows you to uncover the unique brilliance that lies within you. You'll discover capabilities you never knew you had and access the fountain of your creativity.

2. Advancing Your Career:

By investing in your skills, you become a valuable asset in the professional world. Your increasing expertise opens doors to exciting career opportunities and advancement.

3. Strengthening Self-Confidence:

As you nurture your talents, your self-confidence increases. You'll trust in yourself and your abilities, giving you the courage to take on new challenges and overcome any obstacles that come your way.

Now, let's meet John, the master of investing in his skills and talents:

John had a passion for photography, but he felt he needed more formal training to truly excel in his craft.

Step 1: John enrolled in a photography course at a local community college, where he learned essential technical skills and creative techniques.

Step 2: He attended workshops and conferences hosted by renowned photographers, where he gained valuable insights and inspiration.

Step 3: John devoted time each day to practice and experiment with his photography, allowing his skills to grow and develop.

Result: John's investment in his skills paid off. He became an accomplished photographer, and his work was featured in galleries and magazines. His passion turned into a successful career he adored.

The takeaway is this: Investing in your skills and talents is like nourishing the seeds of your potential. It's about believing in yourself and committing to your growth, knowing that your talents will blossom into something extraordinary.

Setting and Achieving Personal Growth Goals

Let's embark on an exciting journey of personal growth and explore the art of setting and accomplishing inspiring goals. On this journey of self-development, we'll create a roadmap that will take you to extraordinary heights and give you the power to become the hero of your own story.

So, what are personal growth goals? Think of yourself as an architect, designing the blueprint of your dreams. Personal growth goals are like the foundation of that blueprint—the stepping stones that will guide you to becoming the best version of yourself.

Imagine this: You stand atop a magnificent mountain, feeling proud of your accomplishments. With each step you took, each goal you conquered, you climbed higher and higher towards greatness.

Here's why setting and achieving personal growth goals are essential for pursuing personal development:

1. Empowering Self-Discovery:

Setting personal growth goals allows you to explore your passions, values, and aspirations. It's like embarking on an exciting quest to uncover the depths of your potential.

2. Fostering Progress and Growth:

As you reach each goal, you experience the magic of growth and progress. You'll be amazed at how far you've come and how much more you can achieve.

3. Creating a Purpose-Driven Life:

Setting meaningful personal growth goals gives your life purpose and direction. You'll be motivated to pursue your dreams and make a positive impact on the world.

Now, let's meet Emily, the master of setting and achieving personal growth goals:

Emily had a dream of starting her own business, but she felt overwhelmed by the enormity of the task.

Step 1: Emily broke down her dream into smaller, achievable goals—conducting market research, creating a business plan, and building a prototype.

Step 2: She set specific deadlines for each goal and created a detailed action plan to stay on track.

Step 3: Emily celebrated each milestone she achieved, giving herself the motivation to tackle the next one.

Result: Emily's dedication paid off. She successfully launched her business, and it quickly gained traction in the market. Her dream became a flourishing reality.

The takeaway is this: Setting and achieving personal growth goals is like charting your course to success. It's about taking small steps towards your vision and watching them accumulate into something extraordinary.

VI. Conclusion

Embracing the Abundance Mindset

As we come to the end of our journey to live a life of abundance on a low income, there is one powerful attitude that will take us beyond all boundaries—the abundance mindset.

So, what is the abundance mindset? Imagine yourself standing at the shoreline, looking out at the immense ocean before you. The abundance mindset is like understanding that the ocean's potential is boundless—there is always more to come. It is about embracing the conviction that there is an abundance of chances, resources, and joy in the world, waiting for us to take them.

Imagine this: You are strolling through a beautiful garden, where every flower is in full bloom. With the abundance mindset, you are like the gardener who knows that there is an infinite supply of seeds to plant and nurture.

Here is why embracing the abundance mindset is essential for living a life of abundance on a low income:

1. Moving from Scarcity to Abundance:

The abundance mindset frees us from the restrictions of scarcity thinking. It enables us to see possibilities where others see restrictions and to concentrate on what we have instead of what we lack.

2. Attracting Positivity and Opportunities:

When we radiate positivity and appreciation, we draw in more positive experiences and opportunities into our lives. The abundance mindset is like a magnet for success and satisfaction.

3. Encouraging Generosity and Collaboration:

Embracing abundance means celebrating the success and wealth of others, knowing that their accomplishments do not reduce our own. It encourages a feeling of generosity and collaboration that strengthens our connections with others.

Now, let us meet Alex, the embodiment of the abundance mindset:

Alex was on a low income but had an unshakable faith in the abundance of life. Instead of feeling restricted, Alex saw openings all around.

Step 1: Alex expressed gratitude for the simple joys in life—a warm cup of coffee, a walk in nature, or a kind word from a friend.

Step 2: When faced with difficulties, Alex reframed them as chances for growth and learning. Each setback was a stepping stone towards something better.

Step 3: Alex surrounded themselves with positive and supportive people who also embraced the abundance mindset, creating a network of like-minded individuals.

Result: Alex's life changed. By embracing the abundance mindset, they attracted unexpected opportunities and meaningful connections. Their positive energy drew success, joy, and fulfillment like a magnet.

The takeaway is this: Embracing the abundance mindset is like entering a garden of endless possibilities. It is about recognizing the boundless potential that lies within us and in the world around us.

So, my empowered reader, let us become champions of the abundance mindset. As we shift our outlook and embrace appreciation and positivity, we will unlock the secret to a life of abundance on a low income.

Living a Life of Abundance on a Low Income: Your Journey Continues!

As you embark on your remarkable journey, I want you to know that this is just the beginning. You have the tools and inspiration to create a path of prosperity and fulfillment. Let us take a moment to reflect on the lessons we have learned and the potential that lies ahead.

Living a life of abundance on a low income is like embarking on a grand expedition. Visualize yourself as a brave explorer, sailing towards unknown waters. The voyage may be full of obstacles, but you have the strength and knowledge to overcome them and uncover treasures beyond your imagination.

Throughout this journey, we have discovered powerful strategies and insights that will guide you towards abundance: We have learned to budget prudently, allocate our resources thoughtfully, and take advantage of the power of compounding. We have studied the art of investing in ourselves, nurturing our talents and interests, and setting ambitious goals that lead to personal growth and success.

We have adopted the abundance mindset: Instead of seeing limitations, we have embraced possibilities. We have let go of scarcity thinking and replaced it with appreciation and optimism. We have realized that an abundant life is not only about the resources in our pocket but the richness in our hearts.

But remember, your journey does not end here—this is just the start. As you continue on this path of abundance, I encourage you to keep exploring, keep learning, and keep believing in yourself. There will be moments of doubt and uncertainty, but remember that every setback is an opportunity to become stronger and wiser.

Let me introduce you to one last adventurer—your future self: Imagine yourself standing at the summit of a majestic mountain. You have conquered every challenge, and you are basking in the glory of your accomplishments. Your heart is filled with joy and gratitude, and you know that this is only one of many peaks you will conquer.

Your journey continues with enthusiasm and purpose. Every day presents a new chance to take a step towards your dreams and to make a positive impact on your life and the lives of others. Embrace the unknown with curiosity and courage, for the world is waiting to reveal its wonders to you.

As we part ways, remember this: You are the hero of your own story. You hold the pen to write the chapters of your life. So dream big, set ambitious goals, and trust in your innate power to create a life of abundance.

And always remember that you are not alone on this journey. Your fellow adventurers, mentors, and friends will be with you, cheering you on every step of the way.

So, my intrepid reader, take this wisdom with you and let your journey continue. Embrace every challenge as an opportunity, every setback as a chance to grow, and every success as a testament to your incredible potential.

Now, go forth and live a life of abundance on your own terms. Your adventure awaits, and I have no doubt that your future is filled with an abundance of joy, fulfillment, and prosperity. Bon voyage, my dear friend! May your journey be filled with wonder and magic.